CW00664790

SMUGGLERS IN THE UNDERGROUND HUG TRADE

A Journal of the Plague Year

William Wall

Doire Press

First published in 2021

Doire Press
Aille, Inverin
Co. Galway
www.doirepress.com

Layout: Lisa Frank
Cover design: Tríona Walsh
Cover photo: Liz Kirwan based on figures by the artist Breda
Lynch, who died of Covid in October, 2020. Sit ei terra levis.
Interior photos: Liz Kirwan
Author photo: Liz Kirwan

Printed by Clódóirí CL
Casla, Co. na Gaillimhe

ISBN 978-1-907682-83-4

We gratefully acknowledge the support and assistance of The
Arts Council / An Chomhairle Ealaíon.

CONTENTS

The Geometer   13

Two Poems for My Grandchildren   14

February in Liguria   16

Camogli: I Relitti del Mare   17

Camogli: Wreckage   17

Ritratto con Isola   18

Portrait with Island   18

Porto Corsini   19

La Quarantena   21

Dream   22

Flight to Ireland   23

The Virus   24

We Listen to the News   26

Last Night's Wrack   27

The Crisis   28

The President of the United States of America Mr Donald Trump Visits the Centers for Disease Control and Prevention During the COVID-19 Pandemic and Says   29

In the House of the Dead   30

The Book of Kells   31

The Sky Lifts   32

Postcard   33

The Ides of March   34

Malthus   35

Two Girls Boxing   37

Messages from Italian Friends   38

The Cancellations   40

The Hermit   43

The Beach   44

Lockdown   47

The Silent Road   49

Time in the Pandemic   51

The Strand at Camogli Empty Because of the Pandemic   54

Montale Addresses the Sea of His Memory   55

And How Could We Poets Sing   56

Decameron   57

Two Robins Fighting   58

The Numbers   59

And We Have No Government   60

In These Times   62

Planting   64

Images of the Virus   66

A Pair of Blue Eggs   67

In the City   68

In the Spring Evening   69

In Time of Quarantine   70

The Dialectic of Disease   71

At the Old Helicopter Pad   73

Someone in My English Family   75

The Loss Adjuster   76

Qual Loco d'Inferno   77

Remembering When We Could Sail to Europe   78

Bad Luck   81

Gramsci's Ashes   82

The Silences of the World   84

Cocoon   86

Three Hundred Years   89

Four Fragments of Heraclitus   90

When the Tree Breaks   92

If the Mind is a Machine Nobody Knows Its Parts   93

All Month Long   94

You Walk Away   96

In Memoriam   99

In the Declining Evening I Swim   100

The Receiver of Wreck   103

Everybody Knows   106

Travel Advisory   107

Montale's Prayer for Colour   109

On Reading a Book about Pound   110

I Seem to Have Outlived 112

We Read *The Inferno* at the Beach 117

Trump in Hospital 118

Even the Orcas 119

Rua 120

Who's the Boss Here? 122

The October Lockdown 125

In the In-Between 126

Rapunzel After the Plague 127

Election Days USA 129

Nanjing Residency 130

Duty 134

Defenestration 135

The Bill of Mortality 136

Comrade Robin 138

Like Starlings 139

Minos in Winter 140

The Jewish Cemetery   141

Cast Out Your Dead, The Carcass-Carrier Cries   142

The First Vaccine   143

The Bodies   144

Solstice   145

Christmas   146

In My Invincible Summer   147

O You Who Come to This House of Pain   148

Video Reading Scan Codes   152

Notes   153

Acknowledgements   158

About the Author   159

For the living and the dead of 2020

O you who come to this house of pain
watch where you go and in whom you trust
don't let our glorious entrance
mislead you

— Dante, *Inferno, Canto V*

The Geometer

no straight lines in nature
they say
but one icy morning
at the turning of the year
you take your camera hunting
and come home with ice-triangles
scalene isosceles
and right-angled
inlaid in straight lines
among random stubble spikes

they glow on your screen
the colour of sky and water
and in the underworld
beneath the crystal plates
the dark gaze of the turning earth
eyeing you through the lens
seeing you in the cage
of a perfect geometric shape

January 19th 2020
Cork

Two Poems for My Grandchildren

for Odhran not going on a bear hunt

my not going on a bear hunt
tonight dad Odhran says
his small face pale
in his pale blue onesie
such a busy day
and now there be books
and small grey eyes gazing
at the unstarred firmament

of a bedroom ceiling
and somewhere a bear
is dreaming of glory
the days when little boys and bears
and scary caves
were in the same story

for Ruán on his search

foraging for stones
the evening light sustains Ruán
shells and bits of glass
pirate treasure is uncertain
there are signs but then
a billion stones to hide it
the weight of continents
as light as a seagull's bones

and he comes along the ridge
five years old and full of time
I found the perfect stone
he says showing a clay triangle
on one side blue as sky
and on the other white as lime

February 14th
Camogli, Liguria

February in Liguria

brings early mimosa
the mountain splashed acid yellow
we take it indoors
tame it in a vase

the partisans brought it
down from the mountains
and gave it away
in April '45

they captured a German division
but not with flowers
only hearts
fall to mimosa

February 15th

Camogli: I Relitti del Mare

il gabbiano
del porto
mi guarda
con l'occhio
giallo rosso
il suo disprezzo
lo riconosco
come un politico
si interessa
della vita complessa
della perduta gente
il porto porta i relitti
c'è sempre carne
in quello sguardo
siamo tutti uguali
il turista come
il bambino disperso

Camogli: Wreckage

the seagull
that haunts the port
keeps watch on me
with his yellow-red eyes
I recognise
his disdain
like a politician
he interests himself
in the complex lives
of the damned
the port brings
wreckage to him
there is always flesh
in his regard
we are all equal
the tourist
or the lost child

February 17th
Camogli

Ritratto con Isola

a Vivian Lamarque

oggi dietro di te
ho messo un isolotto
con un uliveto ricco e macchiato
di virgole nere
sopra un mare condizionale
come un occhio
nero-blu che osserva
il cielo con ironia
uno sguardo insistente

e in primo piano
il tuo sorriso
che guarda l'isola
immaginata
come un pastore
di metafore

Portrait with Island

for Vivian Lamarque

today I have put a little
island behind you
an olive grove rich and
speckled with black commas
over a conditional sea
like a dark blue
eye watching
the sky ironically
an insistent gaze

and in the foreground
your big smile
which sees
the imaginary island
like a shepherd
of metaphor

February 18th

Porto Corsini

from the pier at Porto Corsini
we leave the open sea
a voyage to the interior

that weaves a gleaming
basketwork of memory
and forgetting

beyond the pines and roots
flexing through earthen paths
the marsh unfolds
its unchanging universe

only the heron breaks
the torpor of water
and the liquid vowels of birds
sing the pallid weather

of exile they sing
evoking the longing
for the time when we were kings

after the Italian of Daniele Serafini

February 22nd

In the evening home to supper; and there, to my great trouble, hear that the plague is come into the City... but where should it begin but in my good friend and neighbour's, Dr. Burnett, in Fanchurch Street: which in both points troubles me mightily.

— *Diary of Samuel Pepys*

La Quarantena

last night they sent the army
to quarantine Codogno
roadblocks on all the roads
in a shoe shop yesterday
the woman said
Codogno is a beautiful place
but the plague is out
no holding it now

in Florence in 1630
they traced the chicken vendor
and his family
they traced his contacts
they closed the border
and still it came
the plague is out
no holding it now

the streets are silent
no hugs no handshakes
the air heavy with dread
not a puff of wind
rain over the mountain
and snow in the high valleys
the plague is out
no holding it now

February 24th

Dream

I dreamed of tasting blood
in some old war of which we
were the remaining wounded

and woke to hear
the street filled with the to-and-fro
of stretcher-bearers

a thousand personal ambulances
carrying the dead for me
on a bad night we miss our chances

find ourselves left behind
as the front passes
night's fifth column hiding in the light

February 25th

Flight to Ireland

we are fleeing the epidemic
like frightened peasants abandoning everything
conscious of all our antecedents
heading for the hills

a few days ago they sent the army in
the city of Codogno under iron quarantine
we do not know what to expect
as we wait in the little railway station
bound for Rome on a *Freccia Bianca*

and on the train we all avoid each other
and the *capotreno* works the aisles
with a disinfectant spray
we flash through Genoa
whose ships they say brought the Black Death
the song of flight is the noise of the tracks

Rome is half deserted
under the Spanish Steps
strollers are outnumbered by police
the Trevi is still mobbed
we walk the almost empty Corso

a moment of nervous embrace
when we meet our friends
what if we have the infection
what if we pass it on

February 26th

The Virus

in the almost empty airport
masked ones wait for doom
they gaze at their phones
like heroes to the oracle
the numbers rising hour by hour
inexorable as a spring tide
some have seen roadblocks
the army waving them down
some have come by train
every traveller masked
how did we get this far
we wash our hands
and wash them again
we have not seen hands so clean
since Pontius Pilate
we touch nothing
friends and acquaintances
greet with polite nods
no hugging no kissing
no holding hands
this is our future
soon we will gaze at the world
through hazmat eyeglass
listen only to our earbuds
the sweet sound of fear
at eighty decibels

February 26th
Fiumicino Airport,
Rome

Some were of a more barbarous, though, peradventure, a surer way of thinking, avouching that there was no remedy against pestilences better than—no, nor any so good as—to flee before them; wherefore, moved by this reasoning and recking of nought but themselves, very many, both men and women, abandoned their own city, their own houses and homes, their kinsfolk and possessions, and sought the country seats of others, or, at the least, their own, as if the wrath of God, being moved to punish the iniquity of mankind, would not proceed to do so wheresoever they might be, but would content itself with afflicting those only who were found within the walls of their city, or as if they were persuaded that no person was to remain therein and that its last hour was come.

— Giovanni Boccaccio, *Decameron, Day the First*

We Listen to the News

with anxious anticipation
the latest mortality figures from Italy
the good news from China
no new cases in Wuhan
the World Health Organisation
the shortage of isolation beds

we squeeze orange juice
for our immune systems
eat green vegetables
wash our hands with increasing
frequency and vigour
take the sun when there is sun

but today a great bolt of rain
between us and the beeches
unfurls its dark inversion
you stretch and light the lamp
fingers between the pages of your book
no point in being in the dark you say

March 1ˢᵗ
Cork

Last Night's Wrack

last night's wrack of dragon-headed kelp
a thousand blackened carcasses
a wave against the early morning sun
we have driven down to catch the light
on bare sand and broken boats
and have caught ourselves unawares
overwhelmed by
the profusion of decay

we stand in the wind on the cliff-top
and feel ourselves pitching quietly out
so slowly we think
gravity is an end in itself
a kind of beauty
kiss me or we're lost you cry
with heavy hearts we'll fall
down among the dragons

March 2nd

The Crisis

night duty a week ago
I did not sleep for waiting
the word from microbiology
a swab on the first suspected
case in our hospital
what it would mean for us
my fear for one single case
seems utterly ridiculous now
now that we are growing in it

now it is war
a barrage by day and by night
they come to the emergency room
one by one
this is not a bad flu
in two years I have learned
that the people of Bergamo
do not come to the emergency room at all
they did well this time too
they followed all the advice
a week or ten days at home with a fever
without going out
and risking contagion
but now they can't breathe
they need oxygen
they come to us

now is the tragedy of beds
the wards that we emptied fill
the boards with the names of the patients
in different colours
depending on the unit they belong to
all red now
there is only one diagnosis
which is always the same damn thing
bilateral interstitial pneumonia

March 6th

The President of the United States of America Mr Donald Trump Visits the Centers for Disease Control and Prevention During the COVID-19 Pandemic and Says

my uncle was a great person
he taught at MIT
he was at MIT for I think like
a record number of years
he was a great
supergenius
Dr John Trump

I like this stuff
I really get it
people are surprised
that I understand it
every one of these doctors
said how do you know
so much about this

maybe I have a natural ability
maybe I should have done that
instead of running
for president

March 7th

In the House of the Dead

in the house of the dead they are silent
they are cracking bones
the mind is the pain
heartbeat is wheels over cobbles
I hear myself coughing or praying
the ivy flaps on the window

even in this city the wind rouses the dead
they change places constantly
but over the sound of wind
I can hear a heartbeat and fear it is mine
hurry hurry she said there is still time

March 10th

The Book of Kells

they closed the Book of Kells today
some kind of finality

the noise was heard in the old library
twelve hundred years

of silence starting again
in principio erat verbum verum

and in the west a red sunset
a rainbow against the clouds

and in Codogno in Lombardy
no new cases have been reported

even that distant sigh of relief
is something to hold onto this evening

March 10th

The Sky Lifts

the sky lifts on a brittle morning
daffodils shiver
around our single birch

America has closed the gate
Trump blames the EU
our first death was yesterday

China is sending a million
masks to Italy
shamrock is what we send

a buzzard stalls
along the back hedge
watching for unwary animals

we hear his harsh *reeeaak*
even behind our locked down
double-glazed unbreakable glass

March 12th

Postcard

I write to you from a place I don't recognise,
where it seems the winds regenerate
in the corners of houses and the moon
is a headlight covered in insects,
a place free of all precedent,
where the postal stamp is something I sketched,
the plain is a stylistic invention
and anguish is a cartographic concept.
If you were here now it would infuriate you
because in writing I have conceded
that a like place exists, but don't worry
I will escape also from this postcard:
      on the reverse I found the map
      which leads to another dimension.

after the Italian of Federico Italiano

March 13th

The Ides of March

today is your birthday
and the day dawns bright
and bird-filled
bullfinches stripping
early flowers from the plum
a goldfinch's garish flash
when the rain comes
it falls as soft as ash and is gone
a clearing is coming they say
already the west is lighter

the news continues bad
we message the children
strangers send love
we remake old contacts
and avoid old friends and relatives
on the beach we all wave
but avoid salutation
we turn away
in case the spring breeze
carries contagion

March 15th

Malthus

my great-grandfather
remembered
Black '47
spoon-fed cod-liver oil
to guard against typhoid
while the people went by
on their way to the poorhouse
the natural resources of the country
a great part of the population
swept from the soil

today they're talking
about herd immunity
two hundred thousand deaths
Johnson says prepare
to lose your loved ones
now their story is
we're all in this together
the natural resources of the country
a great part of the population
swept from the soil

the same people
saying the same thing
everything changes
and stays the same
though England is infinitely
more peopled now
no longer our lords and masters
instead to give full effect
to the resources of their country
a great part of the population
they want swept from the soil

March 17th

Two Girls Boxing

two girls boxing
on the strand
a ballet of combat
the mist erasing
the horizon
is a cocoon
the lap of the waves
the smack of the gloves
a pair of bright gulls
feinting and diving
over a sandy sea

March 17th

Messages from Italian Friends

for Giovanni Gozzelino and Elisabetta Ferrando

The Doctor

one hundred cases here
twenty dead
the tip of the iceberg
sick people
are staying at home
because they're young
or they're fit
an even greater number
in self-isolation
the problem is
we test only
the symptomatic
in fact only those
who are really unwell
we are short of everything
from swabs
to protective clothing
in Italy
eight per cent of the sick
are medical workers

The Nurse

for the moment I resist
but many of my colleagues
are already sick
exhaustion
is making itself felt
but I try
not to think of it
I get up early
I go to work
I come home at ten o'clock
eat and sleep
and next day it begins again
I miss reading and walking
but that's not important
I only hope that these efforts
succeed in stopping
the epidemic
hugs to all

March 19ᵗʰ

The Cancellations

all public holidays are cancelled
because there's no point anymore
because nothing can be sold
all masses are cancelled
because transubstantiation is postponed
pending a vaccine
Christ is in the vulnerable category
five wounds and a weak immune system
all the sacraments are cancelled
including extreme unction
we are all subject to general absolution
whether we deserve it or not
god the father has been cancelled
for creating the virus in the first place
the holy spirit led the coup
interstellar space has been cancelled
and we can now reach out
and hold the nearest galaxy between two fingers
but we cannot touch our neighbour
or anything in a supermarket
summer has been cancelled
because we won't be able to experience it
and if you don't experience it nothing happened
there will be no beaches
no barbecues because smoke has been cancelled
pollution has been cancelled indefinitely
farming has been cancelled until further notice
and climate change has been prorogued
the building industry has not been cancelled
because builders are essential
but all elective surgery has been cancelled
the government has not been cancelled
even though we didn't vote for them

funerals have been cancelled
the dead are to be left where they fall
the living have been cancelled
there is a rumour on social media
that the future has been cancelled
and all official denials have been cancelled
we await the day when all cancellations
will be cancelled so we can begin again

March 20th - 22nd

The Hermit

in the old field pattern
excavated by a spring tide
from the sands
we found a single whelk shell
we took it home to show
to our grandchildren on Skype

it was the hermitage
of a solitary crab
a social distancer
extraordinaire
he came out to wave at us
somewhat surprised
by our proximity
and by technology
insofar as a crab

can look surprised
we brought him back
to Ardnahinch
and placed him under a frond
of bladderwrack
in a half-tide pool
at a safe distance
from humanity
we wished him
the best of luck
and promised to see him again
when all of this is over
he never even waved goodbye

March 24ᵗʰ

The Beach

For Liz, on the day that walking
on the beach was forbidden

i

the beach is an occasion
a skin scalded by sun
a bird-speckled distance
the ghost of oceans
a stone beaten
a cold star fallen
the beach is an
open aperture
a mirror silvered
its future is glass
the beach is a passage
a kelpy fastness
in bronze and brass
a twisted strand of blond
netted in hexagons
a shield and a scimitar
a stony-hearted invader
the beach escapes
every definition
a landscape
that shifts and sings
a happening
between earth and sea
a constant inconstancy

ii

the beach is our past
it burns like a phosphorous flare in memory
we recall minutiae
the hexagonal shapes left by the waves
the sheets of sand as smooth as paper
the marl of the ancient bog
rising through sand after gales
the revelation of buried field marks
the way the sea takes kelp from the reefs and flats and heaps it
the small waves rolling and tripping and dissipating

once an old lady gave me a list she had made
of all the ships that sank along this coast
that ran on rocks and broke up all hands lost
that ran onto the sand and were pillaged
that broke their backs in big Atlantic storms
that mistook the light or were shown a false light
that strayed in fog
great sails and masts and shrouds and stays washed up like kelp
boilers hissing and groaning on the Smiths Rocks
the savagery of sea-broken bones and hearts against the impervious shore
cargoes of brandy or silk or cotton gone to Davy Jones
or lining the bellies or pockets of the local breakers
think not of the sea as a place of sport my mother used to say
she lost her brother and her uncle to it
their names carved on the family stone Lost At Sea
the sea is nobody's friend

but we speak of the strand
where we are still sure of foot
though the sands shift and every tide is change
though we place stones in a pile to mark a favourite spot
and cannot find it on the following day
though we return a hermit crab to a certain pool
and the pool is gone when we return
though the strand is haunted by the ghost of a buried bog

and the cliffs fall down and white wounds flare along the shore
though the sea eats the land and makes sand of it
and every day some dead creature makes landfall at our feet

still we know where we stand
and only when we venture into the summer sea
stumbling over hidden shelves and sinks and broken stones
are we aware of the scars of history

March 28th

Lockdown

we are having an at home day
for the foreseeable future
we are in quarantine
we will be lucky
if it's only forty days
and outside people are sick
and people are dying
while we watch two robins
feeding each other
from our back-garden beds
we survive by loving
one morsel at a time

March 29th

The Silent Road

the road that passes our gate
has fallen silent
all our days in this house
thirty years and more
we have wished for this moment
and now we are bereft

March 29th

No longer were there individual destinies; only a collective destiny, made of plague and the emotions shared by all.

— Albert Camus, *The Plague*

Time in the Pandemic

i
our time is punctuated by milk deliveries
by turning leaves
on books and trees
by the evening statement of infections
ever increasing numbers like an exponential clock
for the first time ever we remember
the future better than the past
or one or more possible futures
time is our syntax
our amniotic fluid
to lose it is to lose our way
to drown in timelessness
without time there can be no direction
no travel therefore no distance
no change and no place
all times are one
past present and future
we are reduced to bare life

ii
in the Chauvet cave
the same animals
are drawn in the same way
five thousand years apart

what will remain of our fears
at five thousand years distance

iii
we measure time
by the rise of disorder
in a perfect order
time would stand still
entropy is god's bad joke

at the level of the molecule
there is no consolation
everything is present
and nothing changes
time is no more
than a point of view
the earth was and shall be
without form and void

iv
everyone feels
the fine weather
at the same time
since the pandemic began
high pressure dominates our days

bees out snorting pollen
in the early morning
a tractor harrowing
at midnight in the back field
we remark the irony

and wonder if pandemics
always play against
a soundtrack of birdsong
to taunt us in quarantine
in this time of distance

v
the days are longer
and the nights are too long
and we go to bed at all hours
but always rise before seven with the light
and the empty roads
and the continuous and mysterious
hum of the silent city

and the big pink moon in the crystal night
and the dawn fog that hides the trees
birdsong so bright it breaks your heart
Newton's perfect time ticks on regardless
though nobody believes it now
and Einstein's time bends ever more
around the profound gravity of our fears
this will go on forever we think one day
and the next expect it will end some day soon
scientists pronounce normality in terminal decline
but we foretell the return of the everyday
knowing that no matter what ensues
we will adapt to the new
and it will be ordinary

vi
the world has reached
one million cases
of the novel coronavirus

and one hundred
and twenty days ago
one person was infected

April 1ˢᵗ - 9ᵗʰ
Cork City

The Strand at Camogli Empty Because of the Pandemic

the nostalgia of live webcams
I'm looking at the recent past
of places I love
coming from far away
with milliseconds delay

the sea a beaten panel
old copper verdigrised
the shuffling waves
stones turned in their graves
and the empty beach

April 4th

Montale Addresses the Sea of His Memory

I wanted to feel myself broken
and essential like the pebbles you roll
eaten out of the salt
chipped out of time
witness to a cold undying desire

but it was not like that
an intense man
absorbed by himself
and others
watching the fire
of a fleeting life
a man late to the fray
and therefore untouchable

I wanted to find the evil
that eats the world from inside
the little twisted lever that stops
the wheel of the universe
and all I saw
was the trivial everyday
as if everything was ready to fall apart

following the ruts of a track
inviting as it was
I had its opposite in my heart
and perhaps I needed the blade that slices
the mind that resolves
and determines itself
other books were necessary to me
besides your thunderous pages
but I regret nothing
you still melt the knots I carry inside
with your song
your frenzy rises to the stars now

after the Italian of Eugenio Montale

April 6th

And How Could We Poets Sing

with this foreign foot upon our hearts
among the dead abandoned in the squares
in the grass hardened by ice
the lamb's wail of the little children
the black scream of the mother
going to meet her son
crucified on a telegraph pole

among the sally branches as votives
our lyres too are hanging
they swing stiffly in the sorry wind

after the Italian of Salvatore Quasimodo

April 10th

Decameron

unsuspected voids surprise the passer-by
the smallest deviation from the prescribed way
an alteration in the direction of the wind
a sudden shower of hail or rain

and the next step is infinity
so we keep our heads down and wait for the light
we never move too fast or too far
passing the time by telling convenient lies

April 11th

Two Robins Fighting

It is not commonly known that the Robin is a quarrelsome bird it is not only at frequent warfare with its own species but attacks boldly every other small bird that comes in its way and is generally the conqueror.

— John Clare

at first we thought
it was some elaborate
courting rite
a couple dancing
with angel wings
a mating pirouette

until we saw the beaks
and recalled two cock
robins can't walk
the same ground
our strip of lawn
is their Rhineland

April 12th

The Numbers

everybody talks numbers
the rate of growth
the number of new infections
the mortality rate

we count small comforts
calculate social distance
knowing now what is meant by
exponential increase

we worry that they're not
counting everybody
that not everyone counts
in the bill of mortality

in the small cold hours
dread wakes us
we rise in the morning
to the night's disasters

and several times a day
a helicopter ambulance
passes overhead
on its way to the hospital

April 13th

And We Have No Government

we have a half-government
that nobody wanted
and they are deep in talks
with another party
a pseudo-half-government
that nobody wanted
and we will eventually get
an almost-government
that nobody wants
       it's called doing your duty
       answering Ireland's call
       stepping up to the plate
       putting the country first
       taking one for the team
       putting on the green jersey
       facing reality
but we all know the real reason
is because the government we wanted
must be kept out because we wanted it
and the government we wanted
didn't get enough votes
because they didn't field enough
candidates because they were afraid
no one would want them
even though they had
votes to spare on election day
and the most first preferences
and anyway they wouldn't want to do
what the half-government wants to do
because we don't want them to do it
and we all know the number one
requirement for forming a government
with the half-government
and the pseudo-half-government
is that you have to be prepared
to do what people didn't vote for
and wouldn't vote for

because nobody would do that
to their neighbours in a time of need

April 14th

In These Times

we look inwards
closed in our houses
in our selves
keeping a small flame
burning in the hearth
fed with memories
and hopes for a future
this is the time when
the introvert is king

times that hang by
a fine bright filament
one moment to the next
we wake with plans
for passing the day
books to read
the garden
the solitary walk
this is the time when
the introvert is king

time contains all things
including space
and time itself
it can change shape
and name and nature
and still be time
whatever else we
have enough of it now
this is the time when
the introvert is king

today is Easter Sunday
I saw the sun dance
in a blackthorn
Christ will not rise today
there's no work to go to
we are completely alone
carpenters of broken hearts
menders of worn souls
in the time when
the introvert is king

April 15th

Planting

It was about the 10ᵗʰ September, that my curiosity led or, rather drove, me to go and see this pit again, when there had been near 400 people buried in it.

—Daniel Defoe, *A Journal of the Plague Year*

we're late planting early
potatoes in the three-corner
patch under the window
the warmest in the garden

with the pear-tree behind
a mass of white and pink
like an extravagant ruffle
something Elizabethan

queens we planted too
my father's favourite
and runner beans
and camomile to calm our nights

ten years or more
since we grew food here last
these days when sunshine
seems to be certain and endless

we read in the sun
coffee on the garden seat
the radio tuned to Lyric
we hear the Mozart *Dies irae*

and I read that in Aldgate
in the plague of sixty-five
they dug a pit forty feet in length
and twenty deep and would have

have gone deeper but that
water rose in the workings
it's best to know your ground
when you go planting

April 16th

Images of the Virus

in ultramarine
in scarlet
crimson or coral
ivory pearl
or sapphire blue

we imagine
it crowned
the corona
in kaleidoscope
a thing of beauty

but I see it
as a floating mine
drifting among
shipwrecked souls
it explodes
on contact

April 18th

A Pair of Blue Eggs

i
outside our door
the fragile shells
traces of albumen
the sawtooth edge
breached by the beak
a starling's egg
nested in the eaves
somewhere the nestling
waits for food
one day soon we'll
see him wing it
into the morning
his yellow beak
his turquoise flash
his geiger-counter trill
his tail-less arse

ii
you are breaking eggs
into a glass bowl
scones will occur
the oven hums
light filters through
the bones of
the chestnut tree
and across the valley
picks out the cambric
blossom of the thorn
through the open door
the blackbird's
liquid chorus
evening is the codex
on which nature writes
we read it slowly
with all our senses

April 20th

In the City

the lights still go red
but no traffic stops
no pedestrian
makes the crossing
and the river runs
on whispering cogs
under the bridge
the city's ancient
history of silence
still tells itself

April 21st

In the Spring Evening

the hill is a long march
a line of thorn and ash
blind leading blind
against a vitreous sky
a fractal of scored glass
the pale sun sets
away over water
a telegraph semaphore
carries robin's song
pigeon cooing
blackbird's clear note
crow from the wood
sound of my foot
on the gravelled road
darkness rising apace
infilling our past
time's faithless arrow
already sorrowing
for tomorrow

April 22nd

In Time of Quarantine

and some of us will be smugglers
in the underground hug trade
black market kissers
purveyors of under-the-counter embraces
solicitors of indulgence
intimacy pushers on the bright side of the street
our only law will be affection
our currency will be love
from which there is no default

you will find us in the missing places
in the spaces between stony stares
in hospitable infirmaries
loitering by the private doors of public houses
holding hands like young lovers on a first night out
returning advances
transported by proximity
no one will ever be isolated
in our intensive care

April 27th

The Dialectic of Disease

thesis

once upon a time in Wuhan
and then Italy

antithesis

they closed everything
the people were closed in their homes
the streets were occupied
by disused policemen
in paper masks
on the beaches roebucks swam
wild boar grazed the pavements
the army sent lorries to transport
the dead to the next world
people went to hospital to die
and when people died at home
nobody came and doctors became
sick of their patients and also died
and the people sang opera
balcony to balcony
the kind of thing
that always happened in the gods

synthesis

somewhere on a quiet street
between two rows of houses
by a bar that serves
pastry and coffee
a shadow falls
good morning Mr Death
we have seen enough of you

April 28th

Besides this, it was observed with great uneasiness by the people that the weekly bills in general increased very much during these weeks, although it was at a time of the year when usually the bills are very moderate.

The usual number of burials within the bills of mortality for a week was from about 240 or thereabouts to 300. The last was esteemed a pretty high bill; but after this we found the bills successively increasing as follows:—

	Buried.	Increased.
December the 20th to the 27th	291	...
" " 27th " 3rd January	349	58
January the 3rd " 10th "	394	45
" " 10th " 17th "	415	21
" " 17th " 24th "	474	59

This last bill was really frightful, being a higher number than had been known to have been buried in one week since the preceding visitation of 1656.

— Daniel Defoe, *A Journal of the Plague Year*

At the Old Helicopter Pad

the only new thing in this place
is a slab of cement
the ditches are as old as the fields
there are wild strawberries
at the edges
and blackberries will come
blackbirds and thrushes
garnering among the thorns

but this was once a sally garden
something useful
for thatching and basket weaving
before the great gale of money
swept through the country
and block-layers
bought helicopters
forgetting no doubt
the old proverb
ní h-é lá na gaoithe lá na scolb

May 4ᵗʰ

*'The day of the gale is not the day for the scollops'. Scollops, or *scolb* in Irish, were sally (willow) branches bent into staples for securing thatch in place.

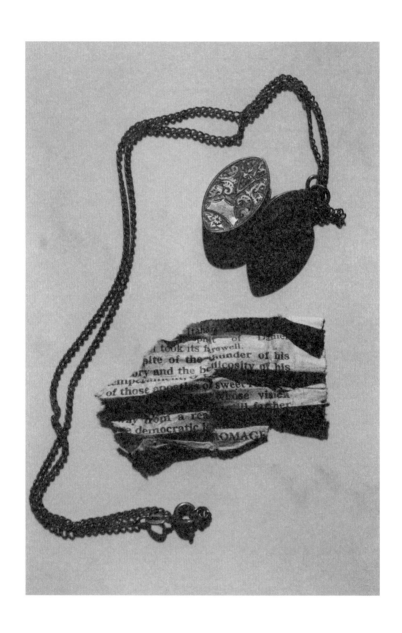

Someone in My English Family

not once removed or twice removed
but removed forever
a Victorian clergyman or a clergyman's child
in the lambent gloaming of a long-forgotten life

like everyone else we are spring cleaning
in the quarantine silence
turning out the past to make way
for whatever the future holds

and discover someone kept mementos
of Napoleon Bonaparte and a sword that was at Trafalgar
meticulous family records of people of no importance
a trinket box of Victoriana

and a battered locket
containing news of the death
of Daniel O'Connell The Liberator in the city of Genoa
in the worst year of the Great Famine

in the flitters of time
in a tin box of ribbons medals and buttons
someone carefully folded a fragment of newspaper
into a heart of gold

teaching me that history can only be built
of the filaments that web us heart to heart
everything else is a fiction
such as we shape to make sense of the impossible

May 6th

The Loss Adjuster

we are adjusting to loss
twenty-nine dead last night
we haven't been out in weeks
and yesterday the loss adjuster
called to assess the last big storm's
damage to the ridge tiles on our roof
it seemed trivial in the extreme
like something happening
in a doll's house
more or less
nothing
really

May 8th

Qual Loco d'Inferno

at last we have achieved a balance
between the private nursing homes
and the slaughterhouses

May 14th

Remembering When We Could Sail to Europe

i

the wake stretched to infinity
a calm sea to Finistère
we saw whales at dinnertime
a pod going east
consider the subtleness of the sea
as Melville said

and the sun set behind us like a scarlet full stop
over the edge of the world
the monstrous engine of time
we were driving into darkness like there was no today

ii

in Sicily *la terra trema*
we were nearly always uneasy
the deep breathing of an almost insensible earthquake
and Etna smoked
the sea complained against the foundations of the house
we woke to elemental uncertainty
a seasick island

and down the road they washed ashore
from inflatable boats and ruined trawlers

iii

on the banks of the Loire
our son took his first steps
thunder and lightning coming down the river
like a memory of war
the lights went out and the landlord gave us candles
in our attic room the air crackled
all change begins in uncertainty
those three tottering steps
in the flickering storm

iv
in the *carüggi* of Genoa
we heard Francesca cry
amor ch'a nullo amato amar perdona

waiting in the darkened door
for a passing sailor or longshoreman from the port
breeze foetid with the smell of frying fish
eccoci due da soli
not me sister

v

this was so many years before everything changed
finding ourselves for the first time in France
without a map
hitching lifts from amused Parisians in Citroens
catching or not catching local buses
feeling we had travelled thousands of miles
because a continent is vast
and we were islanders at large

and later
at home
buying a map of France to chart our travels
and finding we had passed our two weeks
circling on a radius of twenty miles
and thinking it was an Odyssey

vi
we woke one morning in Forlì
in Emilia Romagna
in the university guesthouse
to the susurrus of a thousand
bicycles in the rush-hour

vi
that first voyage
Cork to Roscoff
before us the end of the world
we were in fact coming back from beyond
the western isle
imagine timelessness
our wintry island in a sea of rain
Europa calling us home

May 15th

Bad Luck

the banks are white
the sweet scent of the thorn
it was bad luck my mother said
to bring it into the house

she looked for the new moon
always knowing when it would rise
it was a month's bad luck
to see it through glass

in those days we thought bad luck
was a poor yielding potato crop
or a dog worrying sheep
a crack in a favourite cup

not this bleak in-between
this proximityphobia
this surface shyness
this technological intimacy

this twilight of the idle
this diving bell undersea
this numbered isolated
rank cryptocracy

May 16th

Gramsci's Ashes

not like May this unclean air
that darkens the shade
of the stranger's garden
or the glare that blinds
or the sky drizzling
over the yellow attics
a half circle of veils
on the sweep of the Tiber
and the blue hills of Lazio
spreading a deadly peace
loveless like our cursed fate
between the ancient
autumnal walls of May
the greying of the world is here
this decade's end
which reveals among the ruins
the profound and simple power
of remaking life
in the drenched and barren silence

you young man in that May
when error was still life
that Italian May that gave
some force to life
so much less frustrated
and compromised
than our fathers'
my poor brother
already with your fine hand
you sketched the dream
that lights this silence
can't you see it

you who sleep
in this stranger's place
a prisoner still
still the tedious
patricians wall you in
and fading out
some few notes reach you

from the workshop
anvils of Testaccio
easing into evening
between miserable shanties
raw tips of cans scrap iron
where an apprentice rambles
singing his cruel song
his day already ended
as the rain dries away

after the Italian of Pier Paolo Pasolini

May 20th

The Silences of the World

wild boar and their families
roam the streets
fox *flaneurs* on the boulevards
and roebucks window-shopping
grass grows between the cobbles
canal fish flash their breamy glitter
and dolphins too
birdsong in megaphone
streets choked with thistledown

planes stopped flying
there are no contrails
and cars stopped driving
shops stopped selling
the great wheel of capitalism
which crushed people as it rolled
just stopped turning
and though people die
they do not die of work
and they do not die of desire

all my dreams are of silence
and the long-dead
the silence of the grave
while nature raises its own
barbaric yawp
over the roofs of the world
ours the savage impulse to elide
lacuna is our vernacular
our private dialect
as Steiner said
poetry is tempted by silence

May 24ᵗʰ

But what does it mean, the plague? It's life, that's all.

— Albert Camus, *The Plague*

Cocoon

for Ann Kelly

in the cocoon
you are going
slowly mad
doing the ten
thousand steps
round the garden
through the kitchen
round the house
and mind the dresser
up the stairs
into the attic
onto the slates
round and round
the chimney pot
and all you wanted
was to sit at the sea
and drink coffee

in the cocoons
all over Ireland
spinning in dreams
missing grandkids
funerals of friends
you found three blue
eggshells in the garden
someone making
an escape
your moment of grace
you were cocooned
but they never said
you'd be a butterfly
when you got out

just a few lost months
and the chance
to celebrate fifty years of marriage
sitting at the sea
drinking coffee

June 1st

Three Hundred Years

dog rose and purslane
elderflower
cow parsley and hawthorn
buttercup and celandine
the lawn green of the barley field
and the common woodland brown butterfly
in crazy mating couples
rioting in three dimensions

meanwhile elsewhere
policemen in body armour
march on people with their hands up
who only want to put an end
to the cry of the weary
stop I can't breathe
these last three hundred years

June 3rd

Four Fragments of Heraclitus

i
we step out into a clear June night
and there over our heads
an arrangement of crystals
wired to Prussian blue satin
the air is heavy with carnations
roses and valerian
and the boundary of dawn and evening is the Bear

ii
they will burn Minneapolis to the ground tonight
the liquor stores
the police precincts
the Kmart
Starbucks
all things are exchanged for fire

a rage so fierce to tear America down
they would burn the blocks
the shackles
the bilboes
the barracoons
all things are exchanged for fire
as wares for gold and gold for wares

iii
a corona round the sun
doubled and bisected
and split into primary colours

in the corona days
we take it as a bad omen
like the comet Pepys saw
which doth threaten plague
as all men think

the sky washed out
an unnatural heat
almost a thousand new cases
and twenty-nine dead today
if there were no sun it would be night

iv
in the burning city
the air so thick
we can't breathe
the sky an electric red
shadow to shadow
we hold our peace
as we have always done
hiding our faces
seeing through tears
the uncertain world
someone else's real
unreal is us
the city's ghosts
sweepers of streets
cleaners of stairs
we harvest the waste
of a whole civilisation
we haunt the normal
we know where we stand
call us sweet names
terms of endearment
beg our forgiveness
still we know
what you think we don't
if all things turned to smoke
we could smell them out

June 9th

When the Tree Breaks

Tragedy is when the tree breaks instead of bending.

— Ludwig Wittgenstein

in the ferocity of the wind the old beech heaves
and groans a sound like sea on shore
its struggle is our struggle too
to bend and not break
against the insurmountable forces of our lives
times when the storm screams down
and we spin about in too many dimensions
like scraps of old paper in a whirlwind

these days my bones are failing
even the titanium hips they gave me at twenty-eight
stand up straight my mother used to say
and show the world an open face
but now that I need to bend to the gale
how do I learn to give way

June 26th

If the Mind is a Machine Nobody Knows Its Parts

We are engaged in a struggle with language.
— Ludwig Wittgenstein

if the mind is a machine
nobody knows its parts or processes
do we speak the word or the word speak us
are there songs that sing us
can we know without meaning
or mean without knowing
a cat lies sleeping in the sun
when it opens its eyes does it see our world

and when we lie down to sleep
and thoughts and hopes and fears
retell us in unfamiliar tales
are we seeing ourselves as we really are
the unlucky dip of a half-lived life
out of the broken stones of the undertaker's yard

June 27ᵗʰ

All Month Long

the numbers have been falling
the dwindling dead
and the new contagions
one death and three new cases they said

but we fear the months ahead
the second wave coming
we have passed the solstice
and the days are shortening

June 28th

Neither were the physicians at first of any service, ignorant as they were of the proper way to treat it, but they died themselves the most thickly, as they visited the sick most often; nor did any human art succeed any better. Supplications in the temples, divinations, and so forth were found equally futile, till the overwhelming nature of the disaster at last put a stop to them altogether.

— Thucydides, *A History of The Peloponnesian War*
(on the Plague of Athens in 430 BC)

You Walk Away

On the lifting of lockdown

down the empty strand
towards infinity
towards the island
towards the sea

you are thinking
of a long-ago film
where the girl stands
on a snowy hill

the eye slowly tracks
to a certain moment
when she turns
and waves The End

the film was called
The Waving Girl
and it's in your head now
as your hair whirls

in the breeze
and your feet match
the relicts of waves
in the sand

so when you reach
the point where
sand turns to sea
you turn and wave

and behind you
a tiny light
Ballycotton Island
blinks white

sail towards me
o seafarers
I light my torch
for all wanderers

July 1st

In Memoriam

Even the biggest telescope has to have an eye-piece no larger than the human eye.

— Ludwig Wittgenstein

at the scale of a plague
the death of a man in middle age
is represented by the numeral 1
death establishes the rate of exchange
and the truth is there are few reasons
to imagine ourselves significant
considering there have been plagues
since at least the time of Socrates

but you went to get your hair cut
and his daughter told you the news
he used to say your hair was beautiful
he understood its fall
at the scale of the everyday
these things are colossal

July 8th

In the Declining Evening I Swim

i
in the declining evening I swim
wind over sand erasing the sea's staves
the ticking tide

in the limestone breakwater
bottles of Pepsi pieces of plastic can-rings net
in his sixty-fifth year my father

was already old
his ruined back
his big rough farmer hands softening to wax

and here I am at the same age
entering the same sea at the same time of evening
gingerly stepping on the thin line of gravel at the edge

a golden sea
the island and its light on the pencil-line of horizon
on either side the villages falling slowly into the sand

in the struggle between land and sea
better to back the water
it wears the world away like time

the swollen belly of a spring tide
brings forth monsters
the eyes of a lonely child

a crippled boy
a drowned sailor
an old man with the big sad eyes of a seal

and swimming in the sloe-blue sea
contained in my own broken breathing
never stirring the surface tension

the spiritous membrane
half sea half bone I am shedding
the shoreline like an old shell

and from here the world
looks like a pleasure ground
for some rapacious species
not recognisably anyone I know

ii
a girl in a wheelchair
stares hungrily at the sea
when I pass
at a safe distance
she does not break her gaze
a history of what will never be

iii
there are jellyfish
as clear as water
they wash up at our feet
visible only as a shift of light
and a shape not made of sand

two young girls have
forgotten to rescue their dolls
they float on the evening tide
their long hair flowing
like plastic Ophelias

once upon a time
dolls could just be dolls
but in the seas off Lampedusa
and the beaches of Lesbos
our fearful innocence went down

iv
at the water's edge
two girls dancing a slip jig
their reflection in the wet sand
is two crows fighting

July 25th

The Receiver of Wreck

when you see a wreck
you want to be there
at the wheel on the bridge
to feel things breaking
steel grinding on stone
the inrush of ocean
the tidal lift and fall
it's the breaker's yard
and time is the receiver of wreck

the chaos is transient
wreck becomes routine
watch after watch no change
no sight readings taken
to tell where you are
no circle of uncertainty
you're going nowhere
and you know where it is
and time is the receiver of wreck

the sea erupts like a geyser
through the parted plates
of the cargo deck
elsewhere a rock intrudes
a cancer on steel
paper charts and pilots
the history of movement
is all geology now
and time is the receiver of wreck

my father saw his first oranges
when the Celtic wrecked
on the Cow and Calf
nineteen twenty-eight
he plundered oak planks
hid them from Revenue
under the concrete skin

of the new milking parlour
and time is the receiver of wreck

my uncle Donal died
in the wreck of the Neptune
rudderless she drifted
through Italian mines
the blackgang never escapes
he was a leading stoker
below the waterline
in the hot tomb of the ship
and time is the receiver of wreck

between movement and stasis
the indivisible moment
like Zeno's crazy arrow
nothing is happening
a man on a ruined bridge
another discovering oranges
we are in love with change
in the shipwreck of days
and time is the receiver of wreck

July 28ᵗʰ

For when we came to see the crowds and throngs of people which appeared on the Sabbath-days at the churches, and especially in those parts of the town where the plague was abated, or where it was not yet come to its height, it was amazing.

— Daniel Defoe, *A Journal of the Plague Year*

Everybody Knows

everybody knows the plague is upon us
everybody knows the world is fucked
everybody knows the planet is burning
everybody knows it's worse and worse

everybody knows the man is crazy
talking up bleach and sweet sunshine
bitching and whingeing and spitting bile
everybody knows he's vile

everybody talks about the cost in money
but people drown on hospital gurneys
people talk hoax and deep state plot
everybody knows what the virus is not

everybody knows we're living on the internet
everybody knows we know next to nought
everybody knows everybody knows
it's not worth knowing everybody knows

i.m. Leonard Cohen

August 15ᵗʰ

Travel Advisory

a crazy fiddle sounds across the sky
a bodhrán beats
the gods are angry this ferocious grey morning
we have been doing things against all warnings
they hold it against us
the beings that are the world
there is no getting off this island now
the travel advisory says do not travel

they have apportioned blame and they are merciless
they drowned a city yesterday
and thirty-eight degrees in the Arctic not long ago
the sky tears
and the rain comes down like no tomorrow
there is no getting off this island now
the travel advisory says do not travel

the days of the handshake are numbered
we touch funny bones instead
we wear masks to non-fancy dress parties
and we fear the unmasked
we form orderly queues
and sanitise sanitise sanitise
there is no getting off this island now
the travel advisory says do not travel

August 20th

The country presented a new aspect; those who had survived the pestilence began to resume their business; masters were preparing for the employment of workmen in every trade...

—*Alessandro Manzoni, I Promessi Sposi*

Montale's Prayer for Colour

bring me the sunflower I want it put down
in my salt-burnt ground
all day to show to the mirroring blue
of the sky its anxious yellow face

dark things tend to brightness
bodies decline in a flux of colours
sometimes in music   therefore
to vanish is the venture of ventures

bring me the plant that leads
where pale transparencies arise
and life evaporates like perfume
bring me the sunflower crazy with light

after the Italian of Eugenio Montale

September 4th

On Reading a Book about Pound

for Massimo Bacigalupo

I am thinking of old Ezra in his attic
       in Via Marsala
watching the Rothschilds
       drop an anchor
       in his heart
he thought he could foresee
but Ben and Clara by the heels at Milan
came as a bad surprise

him and his *meigeal*
il pizzetto è un po' fascista
as someone said to me
making his eager way
       to Sant'Ambrogio
halfway up the mountain
       climbing for Olga
I have lived in an attic
it's nothing to write home about

what did the old fascist think
in those days when the truth
       came from Treblinka
Mauthausen and beyond
a fury of self-justification
       is bad for poetry
it falls like a fog
on the luminous images
       a verdigris on
       wordsmith's silver
there is no room in Poitiers
where one can cast no shadow

and you my friend
who knew him in his regrets
did he have a plain sense of things
           as they were
in Sant'Ambrogio in the half light
in every word I sense you

willing him to recant
wishing you could absolve him
           for his poetry's sake
           of that one great sin
from which there is no redemption

September 6th

I Seem to Have Outlived

I seem to have outlived
my own disease
        or at least
        the worst of it
an immune system too old to fight me
some sort of consolation
in the shipwreck of bones

once it was an arctic
        of the heart
the star chamber that was me
and which I inhabited
the rack made flesh

and I was in boarding school
        unbearably
        lonely days
and nights the worst of all
the endless empty prayers and hymns
lord for tomorrow and its needs
we get priests beating boys

boys beating boys
the lies and insults
the freezing dormitories
and cold showers
the deadly food
the snobbery
the crude brutality

disease came
like a plane crash
falling in flames into my life
mornings I couldn't get out of bed
        barely able
        to stand

joints that no longer straightened or bent
everything hurt
            in the quotidian fevers
            raving delirium

I dreamed I was at home and woke wailing
a priest standing over me fist raised

but the mind invents its own escape
            tunnels into the open
            a shipworm
            magma seeking a vent
            when it blows
the whole world is winter
my disease was my psyche in flight
I can't say I regret it

and later they gave me steroids
that pumped me up
            like a sunfish
that brought me necrosis
            that ate my joints
and later still there were other
            simples and drugs
and one closed my throat

another punctured my gut
so I spent three weeks
            on morphine
            paranoid
            and pain-free
            fun and games
in the pharmacopeia of the world

and now I've wearied it
an auto-immune disease
            no longer on auto
            an immune system

that can't be arsed
so they tell me to quarantine
the plague cometh
the high-risk category
the danger is a massive auto-
immune reaction
a cytokine storm
such precise irony

I am a ship
the worm eats me
the winds bend and drive me
in the storm I lie to a sheet anchor
I long for harbour
I will sail south out of the eye
bound for quiet

September 7th

Oh, the people went black. I didn't see any of them but some of them did. Oh, it was a desperate flu... In Graiguenamanagh a young pair got it and died, and the poor curate, he was found at some crossroad one night, he had gone out, he was delirious. He got it and went out. He was not dead... There was no such thing as fighting the flu on your feet... But then was not The Black Death worse?

— Miss Catherine Doyle, quoted from an interview collected in *Stacking The Coffins, Influenza, War and Revolution in Ireland,*1918-1919 (Ida Mine, Manchester University Press).

We Read *The Inferno* at the Beach

an easterly wind blows
across our chairs
the coffee cools
as it leaves the flask
lo there are bathers
standing knee deep
in the golden waves
and seabirds make
their moan or dream
against a steel blue sky

on my lap is *canto quinto*
year after year I return
to the second circle
we read together
holding hands against
the tempest of the years
and the infernal storm
this curse of the ages
blowing round the world
like blinding sand
and the countless dead

we whisper promises
to mind each other
to take care of ourselves
to stay safe
all the sweet sighs
recalling joy
in a time of catastrophe
and the wind blows
and the sun shines
and the sand blows away
without diminishing
by one grain
the gilded the beach

September 20th

Trump in Hospital

Trump is either
'going great'
or in deep shit

it's the story
of his whole
presidency

come back Erwin
Schrödinger
all is forgiven

October 3rd

Even the Orcas

are turning on us
they come up from the deep
to tell us to slow down
to knock the steering out
because they know where we're going
even if we don't
and it's over the edge of the world
and we're taking the world with us

they leave us swinging in the wind
directionless
or at least rudderless
drifting drifting

I do not know much about gods
but I think the orcas
know more about us
than we do about them
and they keep it to themselves
by and large

we are in the dogwatch of this plague
the late cold hours
and dawn comes slow
a pale light across water
the golden sands
birds resting in the brack backwaters
the ochre marl of the cliff face
light bending through scrub ash and sally
the papery bark of the birch
landfall at daylight
something to look forward to
in the turn of the year
if the year turns
if the orcas forgive us

October 8th

Rua

Rua, red-haired
reddish-brown russet or copper brown
capall rua a chestnut horse
bonn rua a copper coin
ball rua a rusty spot or a scorched patch
oíche rua a wild night, wild fierce rough strong
gaoth rua mhárta a wild or bitter March wind
*sruth rua rabhart*a a strong spring-tide
cath rua a fierce or bloody battle
rua-fholt red tresses

with your head tilted like a robin listening
you dry your hair
outside the beeches and sycamores
undressing slowly
their autumn clothes
is atáim fé gheasa
ag do rua-fholt a stór

the tongues of the old dead
rustling like dry leaves in a sudden wind
oíche fíor rua a bhí againn aréir
nil fiú bonn rua agam
a language is a world
the word is our habitat

if we could speak the robin's song
we would know the words
but never learn the tune
though he comes to our hand for crumbs
we live in different worlds

I wish I could be inside your head
every once in a while
look out through your eyes
speak your words
though we mean different things
mo chara go daingean thú

I well remember the day we met
how your long hair hung like a curtain
as far as your waist and further
and your eye-beams bound mine
it was a sharp autumn's night
and we danced and talked
leaving on a jet plane
was playing when we kissed
and we sheltered each other
on the sleepy road home
with your hair the colour
of the robin's rusty breast
my robin my love

October 17th

Who's the Boss Here?

and the doctors say close down
we can't keep up with the sick
a month ago it was bad
but every day it's worse
we can see it coming
and every day people we know and love
are drowning in their own blood
    who's the boss here

and the hospitals say close down
we can't keep up with the beds
we're running out of ICU
and we dread a return to March
we're worn out and frightened
not for ourselves but our patients
and every day we hear of some loss
people drowning in their own blood
    who's the boss here

and the people say close down
where is the virus coming from
we're doing our best and wearing masks
washing our hands not seeing friends
they tell us we're spreading it
but it's not me and it's not my family
and every day we are burying the dead
who drowned in their own blood
    who's the boss here

and the minister says what about the economy
we must make ends meet
they haven't thought it through
they can't give us guarantees
just experts who can't see
the bigger picture that we see
just because every day some punter
from the arsehole of nowhere drowns in his blood
          who's the boss here

October 19th

The October Lockdown

the last day before lockdown

everyone is out
taking the sun
like it would burn out before we come back
though we are the only crazy swimmers
rolled in the sea falling on sand
waves breaking in another world

we will seam these memories
in the lining of our hearts
the ocean's pulse
beating through winter nights
the sound of an island breathing slowly

first day of lockdown

rambling the stubble fields round home
a sky of lapis lazuli
a glass dome to everything
our long shadows walk the same fields
interlaced with random curves and angles
they will walk them when we're gone

we think of John Clare
and the old heath's withered brake
robin and wren
and the shriek of the hunting buzzard
the ditches are spry this morning
but the days are ageing

winter is a timeless future
a hard frost among bare branches
snow lying on stubble
and the alien forms of the city below
in pale cubes and pyramids

October 21st & 22nd

In the In-Between

in the in-between time
of quarantine and not quarantine
the politicians play ego games
and the scientists play for life

they haven't thought it through
the politicians tweet
all they're concerned with is numbers
but we think about the real

while real people die
there is no such thing as time
in this country only entropy
we measure progress by decay

October 22nd

Rapunzel After the Plague

not a grey hair of mine
will I let down
like teased steel
old age my heart aches
so many years waiting to hear
golden-haired pronounced
now I hear but will not let it down
for one more johnny at my door

these stones have kept me from
the land poisoned by waste
the air a plume of ash
old stones old bones old hair
the glut of all the undone
too late redemption comes
when I already know
what happens
when the hair comes down

October 26th

Few, again, were they whose bodies were accompanied to the church by more than half a score or a dozen of their neighbours.

— Giovanni Bocaccio, *The Decameron*

Election Days USA

we have been living the life
of Pedro Almodovar
of Eric Rohmer
in so many ways
a better kind of reality
in which happy endings
are not only possible but likely

and the best we can
imagine for ourselves
is a roof over our heads
a warm fire and food in our bellies
while the wolf prowls
just off camera
his pad and bark
the jaunty swish of his tail

and the numbers running down
in someone else's world
three thousand miles away
lives depending on
a few thousand here and there

and the empty rhetoric
the platitudes
words stretched like elastic
as meaningless
as a great bubble of gum

and the day dawns crisp
brightening gold in the beeches
a thin mist in the valley
the news is not bad
a president of the USA
is reputed to be angry
it looks like a good day

November 4th & 5th

Nanjing Residency

i

for Sifan Zhao

I am translating from Italian
while you translate
from English to Chinese
we practise our trades
six thousand miles apart
each word an object
that must be shaped
and once shaped
understood for what it is
and how it will be read and said
and then the way it fits
into the clockwork of the whole

ii

for Pang Yu

we talk about water
the Yangtze
and the Atlantic
your watery home
and mine facing the waves

strange that we agree
across several continents
and two languages
both of us hankering for
the flash of sun on sea

there is no permanence
only the language itself
the stream we swim in
words are our water
we dream their lights

iii
for Wang Shuyi

granite brick upon brick
the Ming enclosed the city
against river pirates
on the Yangtze
every stone in the wall
has a name

but a day came
when the walls were breached
and the old city closed its ears
to the wailing of children
every stone in the wall
has a name

and later people lay like
sunbathers on the river bank
scattered near them
their carelessly discarded heads
every stone in the wall
has a name

we are terrified
by the sounds we have forsaken
the precise sigh a mouth makes
as the blade passes below

iv
in my city of water
the heron fishes for shadows
salmon fling themselves at the future
seagulls form orderly lines
and the sky condenses into
another soft day

in my city of stone
the clocks deny the facts
the angels never take flight
between two ridges
where it lays its head
the roofs at sunset turn to amber

in my city of air
the wind sings
the night sky is immortal
we hang stars in the streets
we dream of sails and wings
to catch the wind

in my city of fire
we have bad memories
smoke in our eyes
the hills look down on the flitters
of a night's intemperate rage
a city burning

v
sometimes you have to imagine
a day when you can stand in a crowded street
in a field of sunflowers
on a mountain road

sometimes you have to imagine
learning a new language
discarding the lexicon of the humdrum
for a new way of being

sometimes the news is too much
the noise of numbers
the silence of quarantine
the half-life of lost love

on those days I think
of sitting with friends in evening sunlight
waking in a new city
swimming in someone else's sea

I dream of Nanjing in spring
standing on the Ming wall
a future longer than the past
ten million books of age

October - November

Duty

I remember the summer
like a shadow on a folding deckchair
like my father's straw hat
with the hole in it
where he pinched the peak
between finger and thumb

old women in black sitting on the quay wall
backs turned to the sunset
my grandmother dipping her ruined feet
in late August for the iodine
a trawler tied to the wall on a spring tide
the smell of old fish and diesel and tarry caulk

scorching heat in the potato field
the racket of buckets filling
my father straightening his bad back
slowly as I do now
my mother doing the books
reconciling the day
and late in the night her cool hand on my forehead

the village is a lunette of water and remembrance
they say that secret doors connect the houses
for the boys to escape the excise
now they smuggle memories
duty unpaid
the welcome contraband
of a silver winter's morning sun

November 22ⁿᵈ

Defenestration

they have taken our
windows and doors
the outside is inside
time to repudiate
the duality to embrace
the emptiness
everything and nothing
the being without with or in
the identity of self and time
the collapsing of between
the infinity of enough
if only the rain holds off

November 23rd

The Bill of Mortality

a speaker of trees
a listener of stars
blind to secrets
she died Monday

a walker of hills
a tale talker
a good companion
he died Tuesday

in friendship gentle
to the sick a nurse
to the weak a helping hand
she died Wednesday

to power a torment
never a saver
always generous
he died Thursday

never a boaster
never a promiser
never a chancer
she died Friday

respectful of age
never a gossip
never a borrower
he died Saturday

no deaths recorded
for Sunday
on Monday
we start again

Adapted from a translation by Kuno Meyer from the Old Irish

November 25th

...for, in short, the infection increased round me, and the bills were risen to almost seven hundred a week, and my brother told me he would venture to stay no longer. I desired him to let me consider of it but till the next day, and I would resolve: and as I had already prepared everything as well as I could as to my business, and whom to entrust my affairs with, I had little to do but to resolve.

— Daniel Defoe, *A Journal of the Plague Year*

Comrade Robin

first you came to the crumbs
and then to my knee
and finally to my dreams
all that long quarantine spring
we listened for your song
in August you vanished
we neither saw nor heard

now at the back door
you call *permesso* again
bow once sometimes twice
and eat from a saucer
you are our red flag
our constant comrade
our red star

December 2nd

Like Starlings

like starlings in the cold
a mighty murmuration
driven by the wind
winding up and down
spinning on their wings
no hope to comfort them
and no relief

or like cranes
sighing as they fly
like arrows of air
out of the shadows
shadows come

master who are these
battered and turned in the breeze
as black as night
the lost people
and he replied
you know them all

and pity caught me
like a hand to my throat
and I was lost

December 3rd

Minos in Winter

in the still calm of a winter's day
the sheets hang luminous
razors of ice catching the morning sun
red clothes-pegs like semaphores
expect danger they say

turn and look back
the way you came is erased
out of a pale sky
the great birds wheel and call

you who come to this house of pain
watch where you go and in whom you trust
don't let our great gateway
make you think of home

December 4th

The Jewish Cemetery

night and morning in winter
when the leaves are stripped from the trees
the lights gleam across the valley
from Curraghkippane
in the smoky mist from the river
the starlings wheel and turn
dead generations recite kaddish

I think of you David in Winter
and more these days of quarantine
when I see the lights of Curraghkippane
filtered through the bare bones of the beeches
the day we stood at your uncle's grave
smoke rising in the valley below
your beloved city
wrapped in a soft haze of forgetfulness

i.m. David Marcus

December 5th

Cast Out Your Dead, The Carcass-Carrier Cries

— John Davies, 1603

in the city of Bergamo no room for the dead
we saw the coffins going south
cast out your dead the carcass-carrier cried
the spectacle of the damned drowned in their own blood

and in New York they put them in common graves
for many a year we thought we had seen an end to plagues
but nature caught us unawares
such a tiny mine to explode our careful days

December 6th

The First Vaccine

for Uğur Şahin and Özlem Türeci

the journey is not determined
by the end point or the point of departure
every step on the road
every stone we stumble on
every companion lost or found
nimble halt or slow

as much by the road behind as before
the long plain and the mountain passes
the milestones and the turnpikes
the shade of every tree in the baking sun
the storm's blackening head
and the sky's lamentation

still journey's end is a lodestar
in the darkest hours shimmering
just above the horizon
a day will come when we will
remember that we walked this way
that we counted every step

December 8ᵗʰ

The Bodies

empty black flies
blow softly down the road
they will come
to bury their dead

December 15th

Solstice

for Illan and Brid

it is the longest night
and the sleepless hours
pass like slow trains
in the passing carriages
we see only our own
cold faces looking back

we have news of a variant
strain of the virus
they are closing the ports
and dawn comes
with a call from my son
to say he can't be
home for Christmas

the light is ice
a sky like solder
over a bleak and barren land
breathing broken glass
mending hearts
this land of one man funerals
and window visits

gods of the field and air
hearken to our call
ring of stones encircle us
light of dawn defend us
with soft rain feed us
we have need of tenderness

December 21ˢᵗ

Christmas

for Oisín and Miranda

Christmas day
dawns bright
all the open doors
memory in the mist
over the valley
here's to absent friends

robin feeds
and later dog
eats what he leaves
cake and skypecalls
and fires are lit

for one day
we don't have to
push the world back
or lock our doors
we're not going
anywhere

these four glasses
filled with the first wine
we have poured
such libation
as the gods require
ours is the larger share

Christmas Day, 2020

In My Invincible Summer

I walk the fields
skirting the frozen pools
stepping daintily
like an excited foal

in the broken lines
of a wintery morning
with no grand gesture
the old year is dying

through the ice
the stubble tells
of harvest past
and golden days

and the hill rises
like a breaking wave
a buzzard circling
in the steel grey

three thousand cases
is the estimate
we circle the same place
but we're far from home yet

December 29^{*th*}

O You Who Come to This House of Pain

in the shallow days of December
in our third lockdown
the end of the strangest year we have lived
the noise of the third wave
falling on us
turning us like stones on the shore
they are reporting thousands
o you who come to this house of pain
watch how you go and whom you trust
        these are the dark days

stay home they say
stay together by staying apart
go masked in the streets
we are all unclean
and a year ago we knew nothing
the last carefree Christmas
the sound of children's laughter
the house of joy
watch how you go and whom you trust
        these are the dark days

photos of last year
need carbon dating
the archaeology of embrace
a handshake petrified in monochrome
a fossilised smile
the beating of heart on heart
only detectable in distortions
in the earth's magnetic field
watch how you go and whom you trust
        these are the dark days

a terrain in 2020 vision
stratified by nightmare
our self-possession lost
among the coffins
leaving Bergamo in army trucks
the sterile neverland of ICU
the battery of hacking coughs
the belling of the pulse oximeter
watch how you go and whom you trust
   these are the dark days

smoke blows down the valley
we're close to zero
and the ground is freezing hard
nature is reckless of our pain
the sun reels and the cold moon follows
and spring will follow winter as of yore
the starlings turn and turn
no refuge only less pain
no hope to comfort them
watch whom you trust and how you go
   these are the dark days

December 31st

Finally, in the depth of winter I learned that there was in me an invincible summer.

— Albert Camus, *Return to Tipasa*

VIDEO READING SCAN CODES

Aim the camera on your digital device to activate the scan codes below.

'Two Poems for
My Grandchildren'
(page 14)

'The Beach'
(page 44)

'In the Spring Evening'
(page 69)

'In Time of Quarantine'
(page 44)

'You Walk Away'
(page 96)

'The Receiver of Wreck'
(page 103)

NOTES

I began this book in February 2020 at the urging of my wife, Liz. She argued that I should somehow attempt to chronicle the experience of living through a pandemic and that such a chronicle might be of interest to future generations. No doubt, many other writers are doing the same thing. My hope is that this 'journal' in the form of poetry will add to what must surely become a mass of observations, notes, diaries, fictions and other literary and artistic representations of this terrible time.

On January 31st 2020 the Italian government announced the first confirmed cases of the virus on Italian soil—two Chinese tourists who were, by then, in hospital in Rome. They would eventually recover and go home.

p. 28 'The Crisis': This poem is based on my translation of an article by Dr Daniele Macchini, a consultant at the Humanitas Gavazzeni Hospital in Bergamo.

p. 31 'The Book of Kells': 'in principio erat verbum verum' 'In the beginning was the true Word', is the opening phrase of the text of *The Book of Cells* (a translation from the Greek of St John's Gospel), one of Ireland's most beautiful illustrated manuscripts.

p. 32 'The Sky Lifts': On March 12th The Irish government announced the closure of creches, schools and universities as well as all public cultural institutions. People were advised to self-isolate as far as possible and to practise 'social distancing' —keeping one metre between people at all times.

p. 35 'Malthus': It was clear from speeches and interviews given by the Prime Minister of England, Boris Johnson, that a sort of laissez-faire policy had been agreed by the British Government in which the virus could 'move through the population' infecting at least 60% of the population to achieve 'herd immunity'. He reversed that decision when a study by Imperial College London pointed out that it would involve the deaths of half a million people, primarily the elderly. Many critics referred to it as a 'cull' and references to Malthus began to surface again in public discourse.

p. 56 'And How Could We Poets Sing': This is a free translation of 'Alle Frondi Dei Salici' (Among the sally branches) by Salvatore Quasimodo. Quasimodo wrote the poem in Milan at the time when the Italian government under Badoglio had surrendered to the Allies and when the Nazis were occupying Milan as part of the so-called Italian Social Republic. This was a time of Nazi massacres and resistance attacks followed by mass punishments. In this instance the plague in question is Fascism.

p. 64 'Planting': On the 16th of April it was revealed that 302 of the 486 deaths from COVID-19 to date had been in nursing homes and residential institutions.

p. 70 'In Time of Quarantine': By the weekend of April 25th Italy and Germany had announced an end to many aspects of the lockdown and journalists and politicians in Ireland were anticipating that the Irish government would begin to relax the restrictions after May 5th. People were beginning to think again about meeting under certain conditions, and about getting out more.

p. 77 'Qual Loco d'Inferno': The title comes from a line from the *Inferno* of Dante, Canto V. 'Dico che quando l'anima mal nata/ li vien dinanzi, tutta si confessa;/e quel conoscitor de le peccata/vede qual loco d'inferno e' da essa' 'I say that when the sin-born soul/comes before him, everything is confessed/ and this sin assessor/ sees which part of hell belongs to it.' This short poem was written on the day we learned that the meatplants and the care homes were then the chief loci of infections.

p. 78 'Remembering When We Could Sail to Europe': *ii La Terra Trema* (The Earth Trembles) is the title of a beautiful neo-realist film by Luchino Visconti. Made in 1948 in a small village called Aci Trezza, close to where we were staying at the time. *iv 'amor ch'a nullo amato amar perdona'* (love which excuses no lover from loving in return) is from Canto V of *Dante's Inferno*. 'Eccoci due da soli' (here come two on their own), spoken by a prostitute as I passed her door with a friend.

p. 92 'When the Tree Breaks': All the quotations from Wittgenstein come from *Culture And Value*, translated by Basil Blackwell and published by The University of Chicago Press, 1980.

p. 96 'You Walk Away': On June 29th the lockdown restrictions were lifted and we could again travel to and from the beach and elsewhere.

p. 103 'The Receiver of Wreck': The MV Alta, a seventy-seven metre cargo ship washed up during Storm Dennis on the coast near Ballycotton in February 2020. She has since been boarded by various people who post videos of unusual locations on Youtube. In early May the news was reporting that the Irish government was having trouble establishing the ownership of the vessel and hence could not appoint an official Receiver of Wreck.

p. 110 'On Reading a Book about Pound': The reference is to *Ezra Pound, Italy and the Cantos* by Massimo Bacigalupo. 'Meigeal' (the Irish for a goatee beard). 'Il pizzetto è un po' fascista' (the meigeal is a little fascist).

p. 117 The poems 'We read *The Inferno* at the Beach', 'Like Starlings' (p.139), 'Minos in Winter' (p.140) are based on Canto V of Dante's *Inferno* and were written as part of a project to commemorate the 700th anniversary of Dante's death. References and quotations from the Inferno occur throughout the book for what I think are obvious reasons.

p. 119 'Even the Orcas': In the late summer of 2020 there were numerous incidents of orcas off the coasts of Spain and Portugal attacking passing boats, especially sailing yachts and knocking their rudders out. The attacks remain unexplained as I write. There are few if any records of such behaviour occurring before now. One theory is that the orcas somehow discovered they could modify the speed of boats by damaging the steering and now they were toying with the passersby.

p.122 'Who's the Boss Here?': On October 5th 2020, the National Public Health Emergency Team (NPHET) of scientific advisors, alarmed by rising COVID infection numbers, advised the Irish government to instate a Level 5 lockdown, the maximum level of lockdown in the government plan. The government refused with Tánaiste Leo Varadkar stating that the scientists 'had not thought it through'. By the weekend of October 17th the numbers had doubled and the government was delaying about making a decision. The press reported that a decision to go to 'level 4.5' would be announced on Monday 19th.

p.125 'The October Lockdown': Ireland entered a second 'lockdown' on October 22nd at Level 5, the highest level of restrictions, the government finally accepting the advice of the scientists. The number of new daily infections stood at about 1,100 for several days. The numbers of people in Intensive Care in hospitals was rising steadily. Once again there were fears that the hospital system would be overwhelmed, especially as 'flu season was about to begin. The day before and the day after lockdown were exceptionally warm and calm for the time of year.

p.130 'Nanjing Residency': in October and November 2020 I was a 'virtual resident' at the city of Nanjing, China. This poem sequence arose out of that engagement. The reference in part *iii* is to the Nanjing Massacre (also known as The Rape of Nanking) in January and February 1937 in which between 40,000 and 300,000 (depending on estimates) citizens of Nanjing were killed by Japanese troops. The reference in part iv is to the Burning of Cork City by British crown forces on the night of December 11th / 12th 1920.

p. 143 'The First Vaccine': On December 8th 2020 the first COVID-19 vaccine was administered on the island of Ireland. The first recipient was a nurse in Belfast. The vaccine had been developed by two Turkish migrants to Germany, Uğur Şahin and Özlem Türeci.

p. 145 'Solstice': A 'window visit' is a 'socially distant visit' to a relative in a nursing home in which the visitor stands outside a closed window and tries to communicate through it. All real visits to nursing homes were halted due to high mortality among the elderly.

p. 146 'Christmas': The last verse is a version of an epigram from *Select Epigrams from The Greek Anthology*, translated by J.W. Mackail.

p. 149 'O You Who Come to This House of Pain': The title is a quotation from Dante's *Inferno*—'o tu che vieni al doloroso ospizio'. The refrain is also a version of lines from the Inferno: 'guarda com'entri e di cui tu ti fide'. By the end of December 2020 the number of infections in Ireland had soared and would continue to rise. The third wave of infection brought exponentially more infections and more serious infections and a much higher level of mortality. It seemed to everyone that loosening restrictions for Christmas had produced a catastrophic effect.

By the end of December 2020 the number of new cases of the virus was on the rise again, a new much more infectious and much more lethal variant had been identified in the U.K. and had spread to Ireland over Christmas, and within a month there were over six thousand cases a day. By January 25th 2021 (as I finalise these edits) the hospitals were full. This morning we learned that there were only 24 free ICU beds in the whole country. As I write, hope for the future lies in the vaccine.

ACKNOWLEDGEMENTS

I am grateful to the following Italian poets for permission to include my versions of their poems in this volume: Federico Italiano (for 'Cartolina') and Daniele Serafini (for part of his sequence 'Quando Eravamo Re'); and to my friend Massimo Bacigalupo, who gave me his book *Ezra Pound, Italy and the Cantos*.

I wish to thank Cork County Council and Nanjing Literature Centre for the Nanjing International Writers' Residency; and The Arts Council/An Chomhairle Ealaíon for the COVID-19 Crisis Response Award.

WILLIAM WALL has published six novels, most recently *Suzy Suzy* (2019) and *Grace's Day* (2018), three collections of short fiction including *The Islands* (2017) *Hearing Voices Seeing Things* (2016) and, and four collections of poetry including *The Yellow House* (2017) and *Ghost Estate* (2011). He was the first European to win the Drue Heinz Literature Prize (2017), and he has won numerous other awards including the Virginia Faulkner Prize, The Sean O'Faolain Prize, several Listowel Writers' Week awards and The Patrick Kavanagh Award. He has been short- or long-listed for many more, including the the Man Booker Prize, the Irish Book Awards, The Forward Prize and the Manchester Fiction Prize. His stories and poems have appeared in magazines and journals in many countries. He was appointed as the innaugural Poet Laureate of Cork in 2020.

William holds a PhD in creative writing from University College, Cork. His work has been widely translated and he translates from Italian. More information on his website: www.williamwall.net.